For Nina and Herman Schneider

with fond love —

Ewar

July 5 · 1951

Dust on a Precipice

BY EVELYN AMES

Only the Loving

My Brother Bird

The Hawk from Heaven — Poems

Daughter of the House

A Glimpse of Eden

A Wind from the West:
Bernstein and the New York
Philharmonic Abroad

In Time Like Glass:
Reflections on a Journey
in Asia

Dust on a Precipice — Poems

DUST ON
A PRECIPICE

New and Selected Poems by

Evelyn Ames

William L. Bauhan, Publisher
DUBLIN, NEW HAMPSHIRE

Library of Congress Cataloguing in Publication data:

Ames, Evelyn Perkins.
    Dust on a Precipice.
    I. Title.
PS3551.M38D8   811'.54   80-26142
ISBN 0-87233-055-9

Set in Baskerville type by A & B Typesetters, Concord, N.H.
and printed in the United States of America

To Amyas

Acknowledgments

Grateful acknowledgment is made to the editors of the following publications in which some of the poems in this volume first appeared, sometimes in slightly different versions.

AMERICAN WEAVE: *Give Her April*
THE AMERICAN SCHOLAR: *Reunion in Snow*
AMICUS JOURNAL: *Wolves in Alaska*
HARPER'S: *Because I Live, Safari*
THE LITERARY REVIEW: FAIRLEIGH DICKINSON UNIV.: *Acropolis at Lindos, Bone-Fishing*
THE NEW YORKER: *The Whippet*
POET LORE: *Death of the Mare, Swimming with Minnows, On Being Attacked by an Old Friend*
PORTAL: *Night Music by the Sea*
SATURDAY REVIEW: *Table Talk, Classroom, Terra Firma*
UNIVERSITY OF KANSAS CITY REVIEW: *The Hawk from Heaven*
VINEYARD GAZETTE: *Encounter, Seashore House, Forest Terror, Beetlebungs, Heron, Spring Warblers, Meditating Outdoors, Sunset Sail*
YANKEE: *Poet at Work, Polar Flight, Giraffe, Seraphine, Sleeping Beauties, Two Graveyards*

Because I Live appears in the Poetry Society of America's 50th Anniversary Anthology: THE GOLDEN YEARS; *The Whippet* appears in the Society's 75th Anniversary Anthology, DIAMOND ANTHOLOGY. *Classroom, Safari, The Poet at Work is Like a Snail, Terra Firma* and *Because I Live* appeared in different volumes of the Borestone Mountain Poetry Awards. *Death of the Mare* received honorable mention in POET LORE's 1976 Stephen Vincent Benet Narrative Poetry Award.

Contents

I

Night Music by the Sea

In the surf of rising wind I stand, alone,
shuddering at its fingers on my skin
and how, at night, waves sound so long, so loud—
but in the house, where laughter's put aside
for listening to music in the darkening room—
they sit, dreaming, and no one saw my going.
There! The blowing grass lit up in squares,
sheet-lightning stutters warnings from a cloud.

How fast night fell! Detached now as a star,
the lighthouse flares: white, white, white,
red—repeated faithfully, like a heart.
On beaches loud by day with seabirds' screaming,
the gulls stand sleeping. Indiscriminate wind
ruffles their down, or plucks at lifeless heaps
where rib-cage, feet, mandibles, reek away.
Somewhere thunder reverberates—long, loud . . .

The two crescendos meet: Eroica streams
from the lighted room—composer against the dark
and not just he but all that host of others,
ranged around him as Blake's angels are:
players, whose art—whose breath, even—is caught
forever; inventors whose ideas flung up
like spray, technicians freeze for us to use:
in undying concert uncounted lives are here.

And all around this dark and murdering sea
(with the storm rising, every signal clear)
there's form, there's music: what originated

in joy and celebration soars out of sight
like a never finished Chartres that builds up
on gathered skills, with glass the sun strains through.
Though crumbling, each, into a nave of bone,
what we create beyond the self endures.

Encounter

We live where the last glacier ended —
our beach, from cliff-edge to deep water,
studded with boulders: fringed hulks
low tides uncover; giants, inshore,
that stay bald — their tonsured heads
platforms for gulls; those far under
that must be dived for to be found.

One — deep-shouldered, thick with weeds
as curls on a sculptured head of Jove
may not have known the air for a million
years. I'd forgotten it was there
and swam at the seaweed-breathing ebb
of a summer solstice full-moon tide:
shoved off from land, face to the sky,
then, far out, was heaved upon something
massive, hard, and so alive
I braced for a lunge, clutching fistfuls
of slippery hair. Expectant, scared,
my body knew before my thought did
who it was on that plunging bull.

The myths we know (and do not know
we know) until one day, amazed,
we're beached on them! Where do they hide?
Some of the planet's molten magma
composed itself, in time, while we,
who seem completed, seethe inside
like fluid fire underground.

Hope

Improbable, wild flower — blowing
in mountain-top winds, securely growing
in a crevice of rock,
leaning on space;
needing for sustenance only this:
the rain's cold shock,
the sun's embrace —
a handful of dust on a precipice.

Give Her April

Don't call Olivia now. Leave her alone.
She's lying out on the shed roof in the sun,
The apple branches—still unleafed and bare—
Scrawling their crooked shadows on her hair;
Leave her: April will soon enough be gone.

Sun-warmed and wind-cooled, wrapped in midday peace,
She's reading the legend of the Golden Fleece;
The story of young Jason and his Argonauts
Sings like the sun in her close-budded thoughts.
She would never hear you calling: she is in ancient Greece.

Nor would she hear it if experience said
That few quests end as the Greek heroes' did:
Her faith and sureness are like the magic bough
Breaking through unknown seas on Argo's prow.
(Remember, remember, her own quest may succeed.)

Don't ever call her to you—let her know
She may stay out till sun and moon are low;
The apple branches—still unleafed and bare—
Will be in blossom soon, and she be fair;
All you can do is give her April, now.

Swimming With Minnows

Word that the "fry" are coming in
from the Caribbean means one thing:
big fish are running. From land, what a scene!
Death charging behind them, millions darken
the water like clouds going over; scarves
of shadow fly, billowing, toward shore.
From above, shadows, but underwater
when I swim out to meet them, I
am swallowed into a blizzard of light
glinting off chips of iridescence
like a glass paper-weight's floating storm —
each so quicksilver sensitive
none even nudges me: moving about,
I wear a mantle of air-clear water.

Safe in the shallows they slow to a hover
and I among them; I flick a finger:
dazzling auroras flash around me
as thousands of slivers of pearl disperse,
flitter, re-form.
                          What place is safe?
Beside that trembling river of lives
a massive tarpon hangs — royal,
resplendent in chain-mail of silver.
Eyeing the flickering crowd, fins barely
astir, he waits for them, open-jawed.

The Whippet

So delicate he looked, so royal,
He made quite plausible those tales
Of princes transformed by a spell.
Leashed to a royal hand, his forebears
Stand proudly in tapestries' mille fleurs.

Few whites were whiter—swans, perhaps,
And white quartz pebbles, certain shells.
In sun, the white was tinctured pink;
In shade, leaned—as clouds do—to blue.
Running, he made bird-flying look slow.

Couchant, with his front paws crossed,
He'd outstare you, eyes down to slits,
The dignity of cats mixed with
Dog love. How he fought to make barks talk;
And trembled, trying not to obtrude!

On the last afternoon, I saw
All of his selfhood draw at once
To one fine, still point; under a birch
(His sister tree) his white grace pled,
See what I am! Look at me well!

And even as we faced each other,
The convergence was being set:
Home-hurrying car and roadside rabbit,
Dog bred to give a rabbit chase.
Each took his cue, two made it—safe.

Our connection snapped. The caved-in shell
That shuddered its life out in my lap
Was so absorbed in dying—or was it
Resisting death? —I had to shout
Across the gap, "You are all right!"

For so it seemed. Some presence there
Inside that torn-up coat maintained
An air of great, impersonal calm.
But who that was I could not name,
For all the eight years we had shared.

Nuns on a Beach

Under the sun's insistent touch,
the buffeting and rush of air,
such a fluttering of sleeves and coifs!
They try to settle, yearn to run
clean out of their habits—take off, flying—
to someone at a distance look

like a flock of sea-birds on the sand.
One of them, with her child-hands gives
out lunches; suddenly the feel
of figs and apples in her palms
turns her round face as wild a pink
as the thorny rugosa at her side.

The youngest sister is found out
by the importunate wind—her skirts
lift up and billow as the rummaging
air discovers her bare skin;
her laughter—earthy, from deep down—
is like an infant's, tickled, loved.

The voices these innocent invasions
tear into little cries of joy
will soon again be banked in choirs,
bodies forget that they came alive—
but for a breath of time the gates
stand open: nymphs exult and shout.

Two Graveyards

Autumn came to New England today;
From Connecticut to Vermont I saw it,
And at two graveyards on the way.

At the first, where some of my forebears lie
In a lap of Massachusetts hills
And a new Thruway hurtles by,

Trucks drilled the air; the village, dying,
Drew down its leaves, moved in its sleep.
Who saw me, out of stone names trying

To reconstruct lives? Someone's scared pet —
Dog instincts quivering between
Attack and lick — was all I met.

No one may ever hunt again
For just those stones. Even names end,
Rubbed out by lichens, frost, rain.

At the other, new grass — bright and thin —
Marks the fresh grave where my father lies.
(Under folded hands, do the clothes sink in?)

No wife's beside him; years ago
Her ash went into ocean and air.
One brother and I alone now wear

Their web of flesh, to our lives shaped;
We still survive—like each of those
Who ran to Job, crying "I escaped."

Now comes the season to be brave.
How far is it, still? What destination?
The way is through life's wondrous grave.

Great Horned Owls

Two seated cats they seem, high up
on the limb of an old pine, except
for the tufted peaks worn on the head
like Vikings' horns, and the way they sit
that bough. They don't budge, not even
for a dog's bark. One eye blinks;
the head inside its havelock swivels—
all in a piece—tuned in to what moves.

A wind comes up and ripples their down
like wheat, or water; they don't stir.
Widow's peaks make of their faces
masks like jousting knights': we're not
to be fooled with, they say, with their moon-stare gaze.
And are still gazing when you come back . . .
soft, patient predators waiting till dark
To fall into air and drift like milk—
weed silk through the woods, scimitars ready.
No wonder Athena wore an owl
on her shoulder! Nothing less imperturbable
could have watched those Olympian rapes
and murders and not flown off.

Death of the Mare

She had been out to grass so long the pasture
Seemed her creation: with all those year-around
Meanderings, cropping as she moved,
She had defined each little hill and hollow,
Given trees their stature, grass its nature.

Thirty-seven: a record of some kind;
Bay coat grizzled, hooves no longer shod,
She would still gallop into a burst of youth
And snort at teasing dogs; one autumn morning
Lay like a whale stranded, could barely rise.

"Keep her up and moving! Try not to let her lie down!"
Did the vet know what he said? Had he walked the dying?
Heartbreaking the propping up, the feeling in
The shoulder you lean to, life's engine running down,
Breath's coming in and going out get harder.

Her struggle was not with us, not even when —
A round lost — we fought to raise her head,
That great ruined stone down in the grasses.
The grass was all sun-kindled, air powdered gold
With light off floating seed-fluff, insects, pollen.

How still it was! A neighbor's hammering
His new stable struck silence like a drum;
A mockingbird sang without pausing, at an insane
Tempo, as though if he stopped once the world would:
Keep it up and moving! Try not to let it die down!

We knew we were losing. How can you overcome
The pull of gravity, the Earth, the center?
That great creature Earth pulled, dragged,
Mastered the mare down, away from our caring.
Life's a triumph of upwardness, a fountain,

Dying, submission to gravity's dead power.
At noon it won. In the level evening sunlight
(the mockingbird in the bushes briefly still)
Seed-fluff drifted and glittered, silvery gold;
The covered mare started becoming the field.

II

Naming the Earth

How would it change
if our planet had a name?
A name of its own —
not just one of its substances.

Other planets do.
Suppose they
were called "Manganese",
"Ammonia", "the Titanium" —
would they appear the same?

Surely Venus seems more of a miniature moon,
Mars more ruddy and Jupiter a-glitter
for wearing the aura of gods!
But our planet — like a foundling —
we speak of as *the* earth, as we'd say *the* child.

Perhaps if we named it we'd treat it better,
stop gouging it out and mucking up its veins,
plaster no more concrete on its skin.
Name it for a goddess, we might honor it, even.

Sleeping Beauties

*"After a hundred years without water, oxygen
or heat, the cryptobiotic Tardigrade can 'return'
to life."* Natural History Magazine

Insect eggs in tree-bark,
and pupae, embryo-curled
in their leaf-light cocoons,
waiting for warmth, for wings;
the frog-tapioca children
bring home — then leave outdoors
to freeze, thaw, simmer
in the sun and freeze again
till one day, April fooled,
the beads sprout tails and *swim* —
all these small dormant beings
have moisture, air, sun.

But not this nightmare thing
Hieronymous Bosch might have
dreamed up: an armadillo
under the microscope,
with legs in rhinoceros folds;
for feet: thorns. No neck —
an astronaut's collar instead;
long sheep's ears and a snout
like a plumber's helper. From each
(perhaps) eye center, springs
an antenna of curved wire;
two more protrude from the collar.

Tuned to Mission Control?
Alert to what signal
after a hundred years?
Brave prince ever to dare
approach this death-in-life—
and wake it with a kiss.

Dialogue

Cat,
Why do you look at me like that?
What have I done that I evoke
Such clear, such agate-cold contempt?
Am I that poor a joke?

In your cat-sight I suppose I am.
Look what I do:
Invent the legend that I think,
And think things through
To ends I tell myself are fine,
Important, logical, immense;
Wear myself out walking the line
(Narrower than the slits in your eyes)
Between spirit and sense,
Self and self-sacrifice,
Free-will and doom
And in the little room left over,
Work for my play, and play being lover.
(Oh all right—scratch! That cushion needs a
cover).

Now let's take you:
You are the sphinx—
Or so at least my whole race thinks
Who sees you come and go at will,
Play with a thread,
Sit dead still by the hour in grass
Which may, with luck, produce one mouse.
For this: free bed,
Free board, freedom to insult me in my house.

What do you think my sphinx, of that?
Is it for this that Egypt had a cult
Of cat?

You see there's somewhere a great fallacy:
You think you're free; I know I'm not.
I love you for this fine pretense,
This act as if you didn't care a whit
If doors are shut, your food too cold, too hot —
You *are* a master of expedience
But — wise?
No — in spite of evidential eyes:
In love you cry like us and moan
But, I aver,
In giving birth we know enough to groan;
You purr.

The Unicorn in Manhattan

Could anything be more improbable
Than this: the magic beast, out of the dream —
Lit woods, the loam of mind, in a city pavement?
Someone who must have been a poet passed by,
Inscribing him (with an umbrella, perhaps?)
While the concrete was soft, still, and drew
Across from him, a butterfly.

They're outside a house about to be torn down;
Instead of a virgin's lap, a littered stoop
Is where the unicorn inclines his head.
The butterfly adds an airy, woodland note;
Placed as it is, its author seems to be saying:
Here is psyche — there, myth.

Whom do we thank for this unforgettable sign?
Whoever's figment it was, it is now a fact
That will take a pneumatic drill, or bomb, to shatter —
And miracles being what they are, needing
No other setting than the one they're in,
Why shouldn't utmost unlikelihood appear
Head bowed, in one's own street, and lap?

Fishing Through the Ice

From shore to shore the pond was a closed book,
its snowy cover arabesqued with tracks
and delicately feather-stitched by mice.

Half of a day it took, with pick-axe and crowbar
to break open; bit by bit, as cracks
were hacked into chasms and chips flew, light

from inside the foot-thick binding shone through.
By dusk the surroundings might have been the ruins
of the Ice-Queen's palace—such heaps of shattered blocks

and iridescent splinters, but at the center:
an open eye, a disk of dark water.
We look in and stare: what may appear from that

gunmetal smoothness that wrinkles a little with wind?
The lines are dropped in, the baited hooks plunge
and sink out of sight. Expectancy verges on prayer:

if life in that underwater world survives,
let it emerge from the secret, roofed-over dark!
We crouch at the eye that shows us to ourselves,

imagining fish in every mirrored gesture
till patience makes statues of us. Then, the flash
of a rose stripe, the surface plopping open

and a small rainbow arches into air.
A fingerling (we free him) slithers from our sight
but a rainbow's a promise: the waters are alive.

33

What proof they send us as the opening swirls
with dappled, color-stippled shapes that curve,
glisten, splash: the water palpitates

with the leaping pebble-shine of trout. We catch,
keep some—whatever in us plumbs the unknown
for clues and glimpses—already richly fed.

Heron

Hour after hour in glassy shallows
He takes delicate steps and leans over his double,
Long neck curved in a question-mark.

To upward eyes of stilted crabs
He is scarcely a shadow —
Less than a cloud his breast of white;
The knotted stems of his two legs
Are water-weeds grown in the sand.

In close formation the minnows come,
Dart, and divide around disaster —
Only the lucky seeing in flight
A slender blade, a coral eye
And the quick-silver shaking of the sky.

Spring Warblers

See, see, see, SEE? The
syllable slides wistfully up
the scale. Elsewhere, a whispery riddle
effervesces. Is it answered, ever?

They're here, here—somewhere in these oaks,
that hedgerow, leaf-color, leaf-size. But
fix the source of sound, the flitter . . .
just as you're set to, it swoops away.

Peel potatoes, take out the garbage
and one materializes on a twig—
sun-yellow, solid. Pick up bird-glasses . . .
the space is empty, the twig trembles.

Beetlebungs

are quirky trees: show
red warnings in July
then keep their leaves till,
        all at once,
they strip to bare intention —
but eccentric, wild!

Most tree-trunks grow in one
direction — lean a little,
branch out, yet keep
on going straight (as rivals
will allow them) — up.

Not these. Lively as flames
they flicker and whirl, cavort
        and turn,
dizzying the eye. Whole woods are
        in motion,
A fiery revel. Where do trees
learn how to twist, like
        tourbillions on
the Fourth of July? They
        all but hiss.

*Note: Beetlebung is a regional name
for a kind of tupelo*

Giraffe

Mammal incapable of sound,
Plant-like being that sees and moves:
In motion so like standing grain
Bending, straightening under wind
Eye scarcely grasps it covers ground;
Stock-still, agaze, a giant flower
Craning over an unseen wall—
Hollyhock creature: rosetted all
The long way up its ungainly stalk
To double attentiveness at the top.

III

The Acropolis at Lindos

Here on this great bare platform in the sky
The world ends. There is no farther to go.
Nothing moves except the wind-tugged grasses
And, over the edge, you can't tell how far down,
A few small hawks, balancing, turning their heads,
Making no visible motion as they veer off.
Nothing sounds but silence: the village, white
As gulls in sunlight, perches under the rim
Of the cracked pedestal the cliffs make;
The Aegean's light-shot silk, unrolling out
To lace below, is too far down to hear:
    We stand on a prow, naked to space; light—
    Streaming from heaven—cries to us pinned in our bodies:
    Sing! Dance! It is so long since praising
    Set us on tiptoe . . . we have forgotten how.

And from their days like grass—what still remains?
The steps we climbed—flights hundreds abreast could mount,
Nothing in sight ahead but flying cloud—
And Athena's temple, less stone now than air,
Brushed by shadows of congregations
Saint Paul drove away . . . curious, how
From here the ardors of the cathedral-builders
Seem almost as far removed as they, while Athena,
Goddess of reason (and of defensive war)
Springs full-armed from the twentieth-century brain:
    We stand at the cliff-edge of a mystery,
    On a wind-swept stage empty of its players,
    While somewhere, trembling just out of reach of all
    Perception, the unimaginable future waits.

The Great Bell (Nikko)

Low lordly venerable as caves
mountains stones gentle as a sigh

the sound begins and one becomes the sound —
vibrating wholly clear through into bone.

With the momentum of a tone that's breathed
slowly out the sound increases spreads

among the trees up the slopes of hills
drowning even temple flutes and drums

till gradually as sun's radiance drains
at evening is at no one instant gone

and having finally ebbed begins again —
takes five full minutes to tell noon.

Climb the hill: you'll find the bell low hung
in the green dusk of cryptomeria trees.

It is without a tongue. A tree-sized beam
swung against it, wakens it to sound:

the bronze, staggered to its inscrutable heart,
is galvanized into a hive whose flying

protracted hum swarms the day for miles
and all things in its path pronounce the time.

42

The Vale of Kashmir

I

In their sunset pinks and dragonfly blue
the women paddling shikharas
drift like flowers on their reflections.
Near to
they turn their heads sharply away
from the traveler's gaze,
twitching a fold of cotton across their faces.
Here, as everywhere
in Moslem and Hindu lands
it is the children raise
joined hands as if in prayer; whose
eyes invite one into a different world,
who smile and call out:
Salaam!

II

Wind—when erratic or unremitting—
can brew more trouble than
a cauldron of devils. In my heaven
it will be banned. Still, who
would have thought its absence
a kind of genius—painting
upside-down mountains on lake glass,
inventing each morning new veils
for the sun to rise through? Evenings,
it cards the woodsmoke into gauze.
And the sounds it orchestrates!
All those near and far callings,
slapping of laundry and boat-paddles,

bird-flutings and rustles, the ribaldries of ducks —
would drive a composer mad!
From dawn muezzin to midnight murmurs,
the empty womb of space
is filled with voices, voices, voices.

Fountains Abbey, 1954

*Fountains, a ruined 12th century Cistercian Abbey, one
of the most powerful and famous in all England, was
stripped in the 16th century, even to the lead of its roof,
for armaments to fight the war with Spain.*

No underwater wreck or ruin
Rests in more peace, more sunk in green
Than these time-rubbed and rounded stones;
Once rainbowed over by stained glass,
They now, like a bare coral reef,
Branch upward from the valley floor.

Across the great North Tower's shell—
Sky-roofed and airy, belled with flowers
The verger winds and seasons toll—
An invisible, all but soundless jet,
Crossing Britain coast to coast,
Unwinds its far, fine vapor trail.

How placidly the white skein drifts
Downwind in soft and softer scallops,
Over the open transept where,
In effigy, the abbot lies.
Feet pressed against a lamb he stares,
Face to the heavens, granite-eyed,

To where beyond the church's ruin
Our progress is scribbled out in cloud.
To him—the tempest of whose times
Unroofed these walls—how must we seem?
We have unroofed the world! What's left
Between us now and all sky?

North Out of Italy

Brim-full as lakes after rain, heady
with the sweetness of where I've been, I give myself
over to the procedures of travel as if
to hospital routine — and allow my tears.
The train moves; surgery begins.
I think of the saying: *partir c'est un peu mourir.*

In our compartment we balance and sway, four strangers
and I, the impassive mountains that sink the valley
in shadow dictating the roadbed's corkscrew windings.
The huddled roofs, the churchbells swinging, still look
Italian; acres of vines embrace and sprawl,
balconies dangle flowers, there are palms — and yet
the valley ineluctably narrows toward the end
of fertility, cultivation, warmth.
                              Strange . . . that where
they stop should be so near their source: on every
wall of every ravine, cascades — twists
of floss in stationary motion — tumble
and join into streams; the land's almost all stone
yet water prevails: creeps underground; slides,
silver-bellied, through threadbare grass, feeding as it flows
last tight-buttoned flowers; goes always for the downward slant,
jumps rock, collides; collects into pools for the next
sheer plunge, blows off crags in shimmering veils —
pours, bubbles, runs, takes every shape
of confluence and leap of joy! Mystery of water,
water, the mother.
                              Soon the valley's down
to two steel tracks and a torrent wide:
the river Tessin; as long as it keeps beside us

we're connected by its Ariadne thread
to Europe's lap—Goethe's "Land wo die
Citronen blühen"—country of the heart.
The Gotthard, named for a saint, is a sky-high wall:
half way to the zenith its precipitous face—
snow-blinding or cloud-erased—bars the way.
At the tunnel: a monument to those who died
breaking a way through, building defenses
against imagined attack when the enemies
that kill, year'round, are avalanches, ice,
fog. A deadly matter: dividing that high.

With a shock of concussion we're plunged into dark
and, strangers to each other, like cocoons
we spin our shreds of thought—dwindled, alone.
Time stretches, seems to stop, then out into odd
quietness and sudden day—rushing downhill
away from summits that stream and smoke snow.
The birth is completed. Weeks nearer absolute cold,
the sky's opaque, larches relinquish leaves
in showers; the mountain chestnuts are salted with snow.

Summer to winter, sap to frost—one is
arrested at the core when leaving a
beloved, or a much loved place.
Like the childhood game of "Still pond! No more moving!"
separation freezes, stops life's inmost gesture.

Then out on the north slope, racing toward winter,
realization comes, dancing to the train's beat:
these raggéd apple trees will bloom once more,
ice lose its grip and small brooks wake and talk:
water, even silenced and frozen, stays.
What's past is perfect, what has been, remains.

Polar Flight

After a night
Quivering with Aurora Borealis:
Billowing portieres of light
Opening, closing; beams
Brushing Polaris, sweeping Cassiopeia's Chair—
A night where earth was veiled, our neighbors stars—

It is quiet; clear.
Under the wing, land
Makes rigid stains; a grid
Of lights marks out a town.
From the height of accumulated ingenuity where
I am privileged to sit, I look down—and weep.

Civilization:
Unbelievable lichen
To have spread—with its own stars—
On the coast of history!
Inchoate growth, it clings to its granite host;
Can it be ferns will appear? Perhaps a tree?

Note: Lichens are the earth's oldest form
of vegetation; ferns came next.

Seashore House, Summer Afternoon

No car outside, no answer to my call
Yet the house is alive:
The parrot chuckles from his swinging prison on the porch,
A dog barks dutifully in some closed room
And window-boxes full of petunias in white petticoats
Wave — all turned the same way at once, like Rockettes,
Toward the sun.

Barely inside the hall: a small pair of loafers,
One toe over the other in shy child gesture.
Did their wearer just levitate, float out through the door?
A note on the table is anchored with a stone.

Everywhere, sunlight:
In curtain-folds, along backs of chairs,
Honey-combs full in the rope matting rug.
One lampshade, awry, is a local sun.
Bright prints of butterflies, fish, shells,
Semaphore colors from chalk-white walls;
On the mantel, a dried starfish and three colored stones exclaim.

The shell of the house, held to my listening being,
Hums with presences — seen and unseen.
One supersedes all:
Through a screen door, between banks of trees
It makes itself known:
A glancing dazzle of kingfisher blue
Stares me down.

Bone-Fishing

The washboard road through the nothing country of dusty
palmettos stutters out at a dock. There the guide waits:
Tracy, well known in town with his sixty-three grandchildren,
three or four teeth and, as we find out, the eyes
of an osprey. We need those.

In the open boat spanking along to the fishing-ground,
the outboard, full on, throttles speech at the source;
we hang on, look around — at miles of dug-in mangroves,
at sea-water dancing over sand two feet or so down.
Somewhere uptide Tracy steps out of the boat
and walks it along like a child's sidewalk toy, muttering
steadily as water talking. We search the glare, squinting,
and rehearse casting. The tide, rising,
makes a waterfall sound.

At Tracy's shout "they're coming!" nothing in sight
but the usual flicker of molten sunlight, the shadow-net
spread on the bottom, till much too late: what we thought
were downslopes of ripples stream by either side
of the boat, fly like birds away. Tracy cackles, we groan.

Uptide again, pulled by that old child
with a snaggled grin — Charon reversed, ferrying
us over rivers of light toward onrushing lives:
we being besieged by *them*. Four separate rushes
we miss before tempers ignite: eyes
can't follow a twirling spoon in such glitter; just feel
the line zing out, falter as the water fails
to seize it, drifts it faster and faster back.
The trick: have the lure there; readiness is all.

Tracy coaches, croons, swears—never lets us slow down;
attentiveness walks the high wire above crowding
distractions, muscle marries mind and then, far out,
water bursts into air: one of those shadow-beings
has singled me out, breaks for the open sea.
Now it's one against one: the earth-bound
(and hindered); its unseen counterpart, quicksilver as thought,
camouflaged in the flow, the shimmer. It pulls for life,
I fight for my footing, Tracy's braced and balanced between.
That invisible host is not of our world, yet one,
growing nearer, drawn in by a kind of love, is its witness.

Air turns it real. Pulled slippery out of the sea,
flopping about in the bilge under our bent
attention, gasping, struggling flesh and bone
arrives in a world it cannot fathom. We try
to study the coat of mail, the overlapping layers
of pearl but are defeated: they are too much
for sight. A shadow out there, but here, to earthly
eyes, a blinding presence, wearing sheer light.

The Hawk from Heaven
For Willis and Bob

It was September, near the equinox,
And in the mountains, a brilliant day of fall,
So quiet you could swear you heard a hum
Made by the turning of the earth's great ball.

On a small mountain lake a man was fishing,
Watching his young son on the shore nearby,
While far above a slow-patrolling hawk
Sailed in wide circles through the empty sky.

The boy was cutting alders in a thicket
His steady blows and the occasional break
Of shattering saplings the only sound among
The peaks. Across the surface of the lake

Light, in an unending procession moved,
Forever arriving at the wooded shore
Where tangled roots and crannies drank it up
While the same water kept on bringing more.

Soothed by his rhythmic work as by a dream
The boy attacked the white and waxy wood
With quiet pleasure, breathing the pungent smell
Of chips, planning what he would make. He stood

And paused then, in the middle of a stroke,
Attracted by a shadow on the ground:
A cloud? On a clear blue day like this? He wondered,
Seeing it widen, when without a sound

The hawk from heaven plummeted and struck:
A daggered whirlwind from the air it came
And in one look he saw the flashing beak,
The round eyes radiating golden flame

And at their center, the black, mysterious core;
He saw the white breast, snowy soft and barred
With brown, and under it the downy breeches
And thrusting legs, creased and horny hard,

And only then he noticed the keen pain
Of flesh eight scimitars at once had torn,
Amazed it was his hand caught in those claws,
His blood springing from each embedded thorn,

When through his thoughts an agony of wings
Whistled, beat him, whipped across his eyes.
He screamed, blinded, whirling in an abyss
Of pinioned terror, falling through black skies

In which miraculously came a voice:
"I'm coming, boy, I'm coming!" the voice cried,
And through the beating dark, in lightning flashes,
He saw his father rushing to his side,

Saw him seize the wild bird by the throat,
And heard another voice, which was his own,
Cry out, protesting, "You'll hurt him, Father, don't!"
He said it, felt unutterably alone

With his wild choice, knowing that he must side
With desperate beauty, that he would have to bleed

Rather then injure a feather of this life
That had attacked him —life that must be freed.

Like some young falconer, new and ill-prepared,
He held it fastened to his wounded wrist
And with a lover's tenderness dislodged
Each talon's grip. And though the great bird hissed

And clapped the twin blades of his beak together,
Somehow they loosed and launched him to the sky,
Then watched him climb a long, invisible stair,
And heard him greet it with a far, thin cry.

IV

Reunion in Snow

Here where the sands of summer still lie buried
Under a cover white as the breasts of gulls,
We came on a golden morning in December:
Snow softened the rocks, snow rounded the bony hulls
Of wrecks at the harbor's mouth, snow smothered the shells.
It was warm—less with the memory of September
Than with May's promise mysterious in the air;
We sat on a log of driftwood, facing the water,
And opened our hearts—in turn laid out the fruits
Of years to consider, explored our half-known selves;
We moved in a world as delicate as flowers.
Thoughts interlaced like arcs of seagulls, white
In the air around us, flying the breathless curves
So soon erased, the patterns of their flight
More real than the element that they informed.
We saw the dazzling shore, the peacock water,
Heard the cold waves unroll, draw back and rest—
And knew they were less true than where we wandered—
Winter explorers, by summer briefly blessed.

Table Talk

We are so practiced at this game
We play it with exactitude;
Between hors d'oeuvres and alcohol
And delicately over food
We talk, disclosing nothing at all.

In early youth we learned the rules:
The gambit of the opening move
With friends as pawns, the season's plays,
Then cautiously we start to prove
What we believe, sum up, appraise.

Nothing but clues. Scrap paper thrown
Along the paths which we have taken:
This way, they call, follow and find!
No closer than two trees, wind-shaken,
We brush the outer leaves of mind,

And always I look at you and wonder
What lightning struck on some black night
And flayed you to the growing wood,
What stormwind bent you or what blight
Ate at your veins and still you stood:

Deaf to the wind and to the thunder
We say the things we think we should.

For Helen
In Memoriam

Thinking of you, unthinkably dying,
your laugh is what I keep on hearing—
across the years and, improbably, now.

Faces the mind tries to picture
waver, like water: features shift
about, as strange as some Picassos.

Voices do better at staying remembered
but laughter best, being the most
inimitable thing we do, distinct

and singular as print of thumb.
Can one get closer to a self
than that spontaneous bloom and fruit

of wit, emotion, voice, combined?
Laughter's the sound a human makes.
Your body, not your laugh, is dying.

Seraphine

The letters, postmarked Vienna, came to my father
Beginning with World War One; I grew up knowing
Their delicate steepled writing, the pearly paper
From whose many folds small gifts slid out.

I still have an ivy-wreath in petit-point,
The size of a dime, and three hand-painted cards:
Edelweiss and gentians flowering in snow;
Beethoven at Schönbrunn, walking with head bowed.

My father gone, she wrote to me instead,
In studied English—formal as a minuet,
All full of curtsied greetings and "gnädige frau"s.
She blessed his memory, knew my children's names.

For over a year not one letter now—
Not even a wedding and birth evoked a word.
A far-off music-box slowed, ran down . . .
And no one in all Vienna I can ask.

Four A.M.

Awake in the tropic night I'm nudged
by a sound. Inside the room?
On the porch where a light burns?
Soft, rhythmic, not as hard as a thud—
not as loud as my heart—
it repeats itself, starts, stops,
over and over—
something with wings is caught.

Bat, or bird, it is not outdoors
nor up in the thatch: it's here,
by my bed. In
between louvers, set
to catch air, I make out
the silhouette
of a moth—wide as my hand with wings spread.

Blocked from freeing him I shift the slope
of the walls that hold him, reducing
his space—God
forgive me if by too much. He tries
again, but less. . . . then still less.

I lie in the darkness, face up,
waiting for daylight for letting him go
and hear within my own life
whatever it is begins and is stopped
again and again; that climbs up screens
and shreds its wings, beating
a way out—into light.
Day, come in time! Come soon!

Meditating Outdoors

Like some mahout, cross-legged on
an elephant's back, I sit—summer
mornings—and ride the whole world.
Around me, space; beneath, earth's skin,
teeming with minuscule lives; I'm poised
between. As though part of me, too,
earth's leaves whisper, its birds fluster
and whistle, peck wood, coo; it hums,
trills, whirrs with insects. I hear
the earth repeatedly draw in
and shush waves; the air that wraps it
swirls. Over and over my breath
comes in, my breath goes. Behind me
the Maharajah Sun bestows
the benefaction of his power.
I ride, elate, into the day.

On Being Attacked by an Old Friend

No warning. It had been clear, warm —
too still maybe: I didn't notice
the air thicken, horizons darken
till in uncanny silence clouds
the color of a bruise boiled over,
the sky went, the world turned
into wind.
             How then to keep one's feet
and some interior compass — how just
to breathe seems hard as lifting stone.
Taking shelter has its hazards:
when the barometer's dead low
the roof may fly off.
                     Deep inside,
the induced storm whirls up, negative
energy charges heart-rate, breath,
each sentry gland to blind assault
if only on a neglected desk
or garden — flowers ripped up along
with litter.
             Where does such fury start?
What fly, crazily buzzing, sets
air moving on this particular course?

Time comes unhinged. What puts it right,
returning one to the tick-tock measure
of usual days? The low pressure,
the squalls, move out to sea. It rains.

A Stranger, Dying

When the woman downstairs was found dead in the bathtub,
people collected, doorbells rang, voices rose.
It sounded like a cocktail party. I'd never met her;
knew only that she lived alone and seldom went out
yet the shock was as bizarre as that evening's weather
when wind tore at the building—a dog tormenting a rag—
and the temperature dived—thirty degrees in one quarter-hour.

Natural causes, they said, but what do coroners know?
She could have been dying for years from heartbreak, boredom,
loneliness. Nobody's made to be shelved alone in two rooms,
wedged on all but one side between others' ongoing lives.
Dead twelve hours. What was I doing at the time she died?
Reading? Telephoning? Running water in the bathroom above?
Water could have been the last sound she heard.

For me, no question of grief—only how terribly odd
that she was dead and I not; she, an object
for impersonal hands, or a furnace to shrink to ashes
while I put on a coat and went to meet a friend.
Out in the roaring street each act struck as new
as if I'd just landed on Alpha Ceti: could I walk? breathe?
would senses perform the same? And the ultimate question:
why should I be here at all? Unbelievably perfect
apparatus for whatever I'm here on earth to do.

What a marvel: the sidewalk held me on its outstretched plane
as I moved ahead, balanced, touching the earth at two points
that kept changing while the earth turned. A circus stunt!
Air, northwest blue, poured into me—a refreshing elixir;

others, like me, passed; I was brushed by the fringes of their being:
"and I told him," "no, no way;" "would we make more money?"
We caught one anothers' eyes or our shoulders touched.

At the corner, traffic compressing, red switched to green.
One eye on the metal herd panting to charge, I crossed—
gauging with the flick of a look one maverick's turning—
all of us moving with a ballet's shifting precisions,
each mind a continuous film unreeling flash-backs,
dubbings, close-ups. At any moment, and
with what small cause, I might be instantly wiped out,
I whom a stranger's dying had given a kind of birth.

No Return

How can the mind revive today
That moment when a shaft of light
Pierced through the clouds, and landscapes gray
From too long winter, turned to bright
And open sun fields? There is no way
To keep such radiance in sight.

Though like a pilgrim of the spring
I walked in orchards white with bloom,
So certain of revisiting
Months later in a midnight room
Each blinding tree—I could not bring
A fraction of that vision home.

Then why should I suppose that now
Forsaken senses might recall
Your voice, your look, your hands and how
They held me? Sunsets from the fall
Of darkness, blossoms on the bough
Cannot be saved. Love, least of all.

V

The Web

On finding an Orb Spider's web
on a foggy morning

Something keeps connecting
those of like heart and mind —
whoever they are, however
many latitudes and longitudes apart:
they are joined. The threads, invisible
as air, quiver with life —
resilient, strong —
like spiders' gossamer that sags with dew,
gets rain-pelted and yanked
by wind, yet doesn't tear.
Whatever it is weaves
us together, the web embraces
and surrounds the world.

Because I Live

Because I live — and you, not —
Waves that traveled the ocean of our years
On their long way to the edges of the world,
Shatter, broken, against that rock.

However much I had become
Terraced to vineyards and grown up to wheat,
A net of towns and roads across my heart —
I am compressed to one hard fact.

Stone does not stay bare stone for long:
The armored pine cone's seed discovers cracks,
Growth and forgetting generate new loam:
I meet an unexpected look or word
And all but break under orchard bloom.

Plato on the Train

What dignity he gives us, briefly neighbors,
each of us closed in our own private doom!
The child opposite—petticoated, gloved and curled,
wears rich compassion over her cheap silk;
we deepen, like colors in a sunset room.

Traffic, glittering in swarms across
the landscape, factories that smoke and stare,
all our machines subside to what they are
while mind, the author—mind, muting the train,
hub of its speed, is sovereign in the air:

radiates out over light-poles, houses, fields,
transfiguring their multiplicity
till all things flying past, ugly and fair,
become more marvelous, more singular
expressions of some one reality.

The vision scatters; what engendered it prevails,
suspended in time, an imperishable sun:
creation condensed in us to flesh and core
from which the impalpable seed goes out and out,
sometimes, like this, to re-create the world.

Wolves in Alaska
shot from helicopters, as part
of a government program

The North woods' silence, thick as moss, deepens.
Some of the steepled forests may never more
resound to the fugues, the primal clamor of wolf-song:
that first call, arching skyward—a crying question—
picked up by another voice till all combine
in harmony, multiplying chords, and the full choir
electrifies cubs, barely able to yelp,
who add their grace-notes of joy. Already great
Nahani may be gone, her bones dwindling
to lace in the forest duff. Will anyone now
camp peacefully near a pack, enjoying in Spring
small bundles of fur tumble each other outside
the mouth of a den? Know each of a family apart
and be accepted; give every one a name?

Their loyalty is what sentences them to die
as they keep following one who wears the fateful
beeping collar that signals where they hide.
Death whirls in from the sky. Its giant shudder
whistles up their fur, batters the drums
of their ears. Biding its time, it hovers, waits.

What have cracks, like branches snapping in storms,
to do with the blood of fallen brothers,
mates, cubs? In widening circles
around them, the snow is smeared; in the fragrant
Spring chill, bright entrails steam.
When nothing more twitches, the weird bird rises,
dips its clumsy glass head, leaves.

The Poet at Work Is
Like a Snail

Watch one someday
Moving along—
The way he shoves
Nerve-naked, out
Forward, aside,
And if that's wrong
Tries over again;
Satisfied
By right feel only—
Poised on the slow
Cohesive flow
Of life extruded
To its root—
Pours from his shell
Softly aglitter,
Like light on water.

As grass-blades bend
And are surmounted
The spiral cave
Bound to his back
Careens and rocks
In plunges deep
Enough to capsize him.
Poor thing, you say,
And stride off.
When you return
He's away, gone,
Out of sight
And oozing on,
His devious track
A trail of pearl.

Small Boy, Drowned

A spell seemed laid on every attempt
at rescue. Why should the nearest boat
go hard aground, life-buoys fall short,
arms lose their hold? Water was
his world before our own! An early
plaything (sly, elusive) that drew
first fright, then laughter; the friend that quenched
thirst, his skin companion, betrayed
and strangled him. Taking no longer
than he once did to slip from his mother
into day, it usurped breath,
extinguished the world. The inverse of birth,
that plunge into otherness, the crying
there was no need this time to coax
or learn. One gasp let in the future;
returned him to the Great Mother.

Terra Firma
for Artur Rubinstein

Beethoven; the conductor gives the sign
And whether with the first notes of violins
Or later, at a prophecy of chords,
It is unmistakable when it occurs—
That instant of grace when the musician finds
Exactly what it was the composer heard
And when the listening mind, like Noah's dove,
Apprehends land beneath, and drops to earth.
We are in balance now; we have found where we belong.

There is another kind of gravity
Than that which pulls the apple to the grass,
Equilibrates our bodies, buildings, trees,
Juggles the stars:
There is some center toward which we move
On hearing music, or great words greatly spoken,
On becoming ourselves the instruments of love:
It has no name; astronomy cannot find it,
Yet more than Earth we feel it to be ours.

Safari

Because well people never stalk
Such game, nor start such fiery beauty
Out of the thickets where they walk,
Plucked at by the long briers of duty—

We never dreamed how far from home
He hunted the lean hounds of mind
Along death's beaches fringed with foam,
Into dark jungles, memory-vined—

Nor guessed with what fanatic care
He scanned the tracked and pitted ground
For the one set of footprints there
Whose maker he had never found;

Yet despite will and work and pain,
That fleet and ultimate gazelle
Escaped across the noonday plain
Lost in the dust of getting well.

Forest Terror

Morning came slowly to our ocean island,
bedeviled by a Spring northeaster. Wind
frenzied the trees and roused dead leaves in crowds;
the near sea was one continuous roar.
The children, storm excitement zipped into parkas,
burst outdoors: Laura, always dancing
whatever else she's doing, pirouetted across
the disheveled lawn. Small of stature, eyes
like fringed gentians, she seems a woodland figure
but woods fern-deep in summer, not these!

Then came the nightmare: her brother back, alone.
Couldn't find her, he said. Panic swelled
into thunderheads and shot out bolts of anger;
the search for her began and her brother paled . . .

None of us leaves the forest behind entirely;
we never outgrow Grimm. A child lost
in the woods, then we are, too — blunder again
stricken, among sky-high terrors; trip
over roots with claws, hear — through gusts of breath
and heart's clamor — disaster, pounding nearer.
Why forget the helpers who come, unasked?
the talking bird, the wise old dwarf? Laura,
her senses not yet split by thought, listened
to them instruct her, made for the sea-roar
and walked the wave-line to a known path.
A shout into the wind's face, then: she's *home!*
But it was we, as well, were back in the house
of here and now — out from the forest of fear.

Sunset Sail

Miles in from the loud sea
On a landlocked lagoon
We sail under a cloud
Of whitely wheeling gulls.
Above where we skim by,
House windows on the bluff
Catch fire and go dark;
The pale, tree-netted moon
Swims for the open sky.

       Listen: how separate and
       Distinct each sound! Wood-thud
       And block-squeak, flutter of sail
       Each accents the long hush
       And hiss or lip-lap along
       The side. Our voices come
       And go, silence and words
       Equal in weight, the gentle-
       Ness, the insouciance
       Of sleep in what we say.

With wind to spare, the rail
Alternately leans
On air and water, wears —
In puffs — a sheath of bubbles
Then a fringe of drops;
The near moon of the sail
Curves cleanly as a sickle;
The water is raked smooth.

We fly and go no where
Inside our frame of shore —
Take tacks till we run out
Of water, come about;
Unbound by destination
Are emperors of motion.
Sailing before the wind,
We fit so into air
We wear the air as skin
And like children, like lovers,
Go free of time, go —
Bare selves — into
Another mode of being:

In this great clear dimension
The riddles we each are
Belong; we signify.
Our secret, old distresses
Attuned, accepted, shared
We let go and become
As we were meant to be —
Until from shore a bark
Breaks through and makes you say
Something about going home,
Going back. Where ever to?
Where we have been was home!